Piano Recital Showcase

CLASSICAL INSPIRATIONS

10 PIANO SOLOS IN CLASSICAL STYLE

CONTENTS

ISBN 978-1-5400-4159-3

Copyright © 2018 by HAL LEONARD LLC
International Copyright Secured All Rights Reserved

Visit Hal Leonard Online at
www.halleonard.com

Contact Us:
Hal Leonard
7777 West Bluemound Road
Milwaukee, WI 53213
Email: info@halleonard.com

In Europe contact:
Hal Leonard Europe Limited
42 Wigmore Street
Marylebone, London, W1U 2RN
Email: info@halleonardeurope.com

In Australia contact:
Hal Leonard Australia Pty. Ltd.
4 Lentara Court
Cheltenham, Victoria, 3192 Australia
Email: info@halleonard.com.au

LATE ELEMENTARY

American Sonatina

I

By Mona Rejino

Allegro, with spirit (♩ = 168-184)

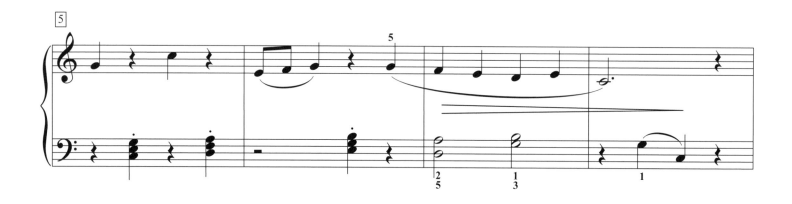

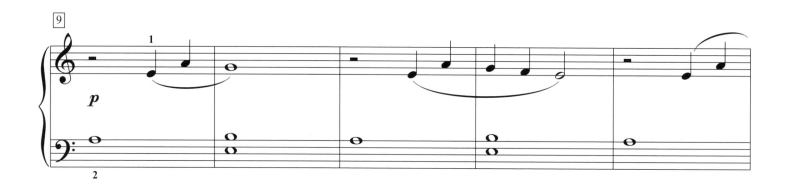

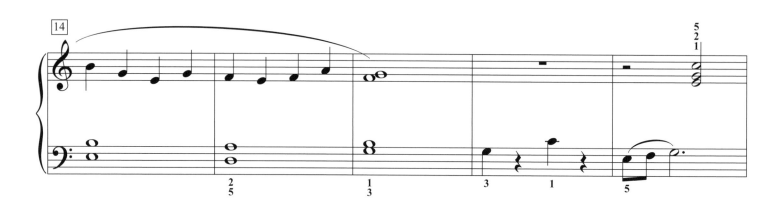

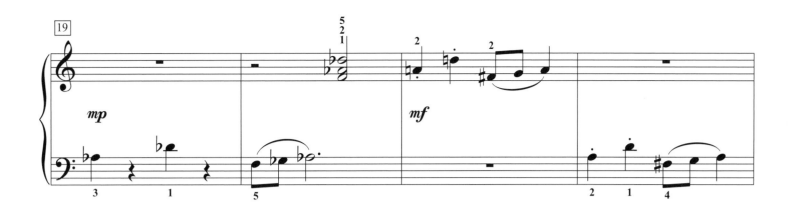

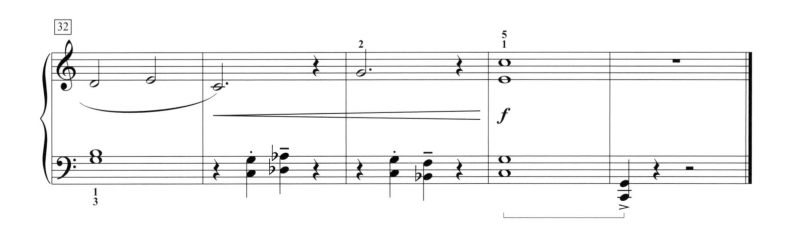

II

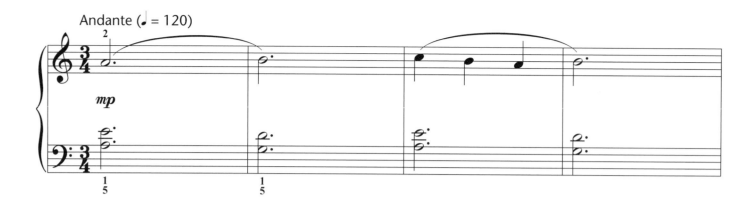

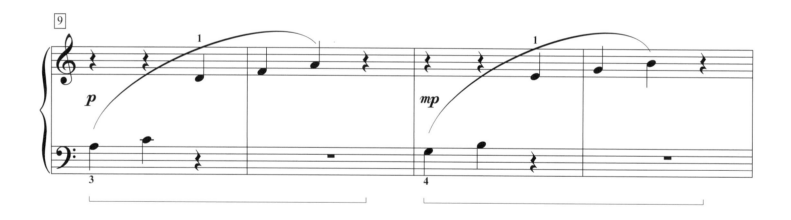

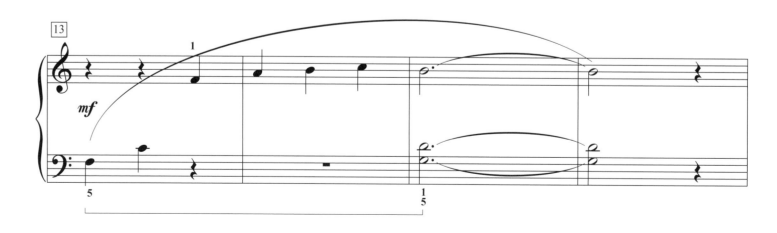

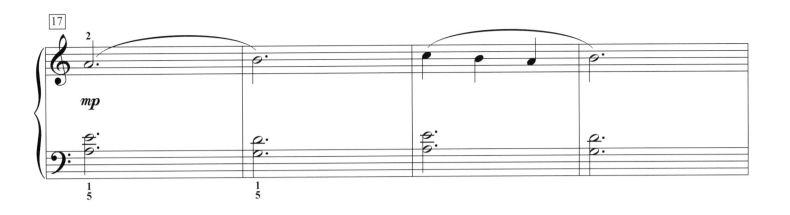

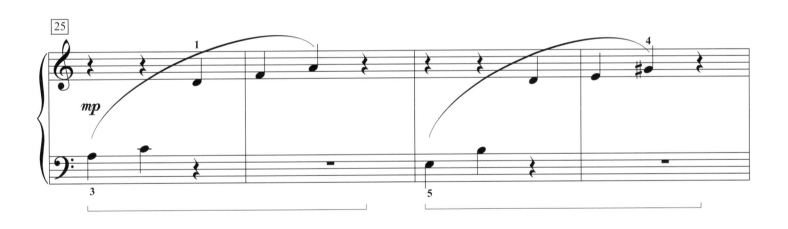

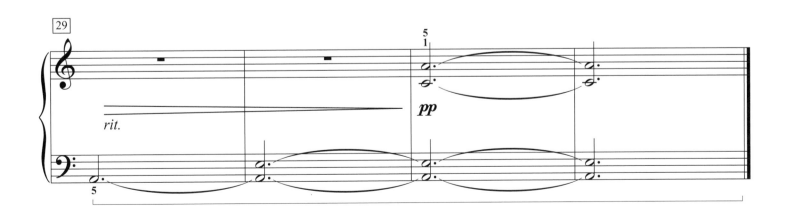

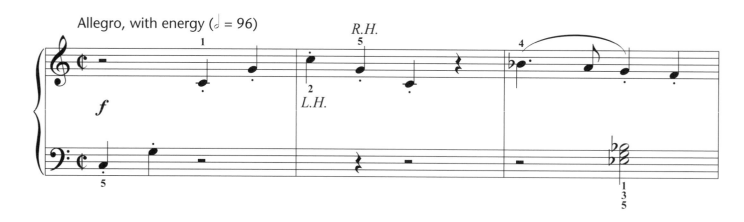

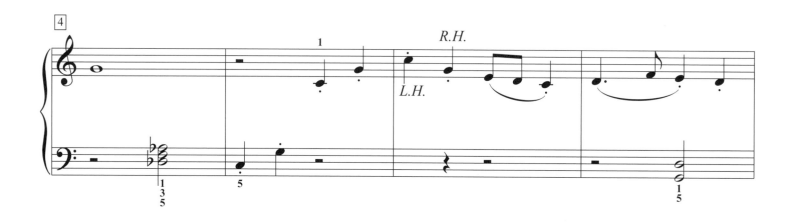

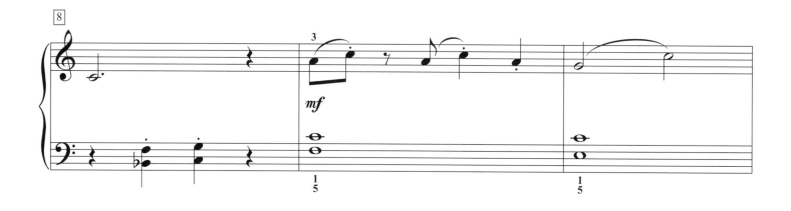

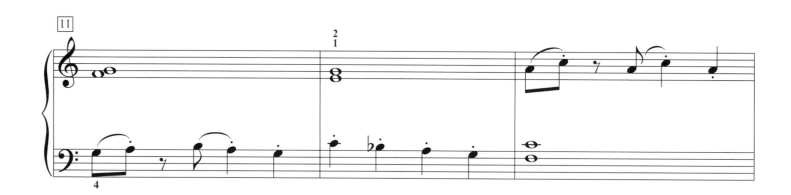

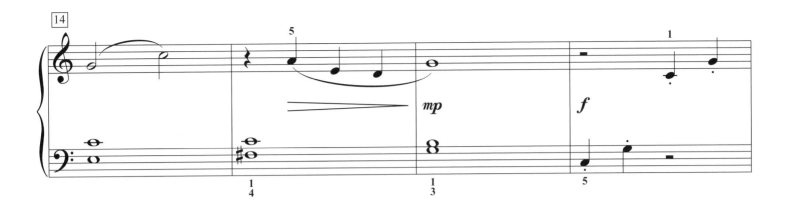

For Emma

Pavane

By Eugénie Rocherolle

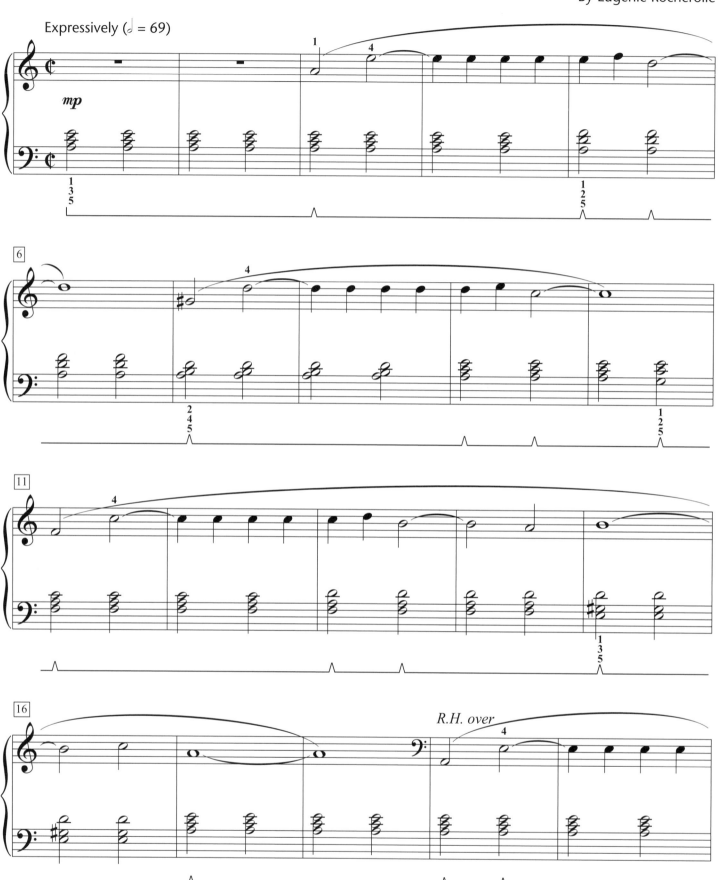

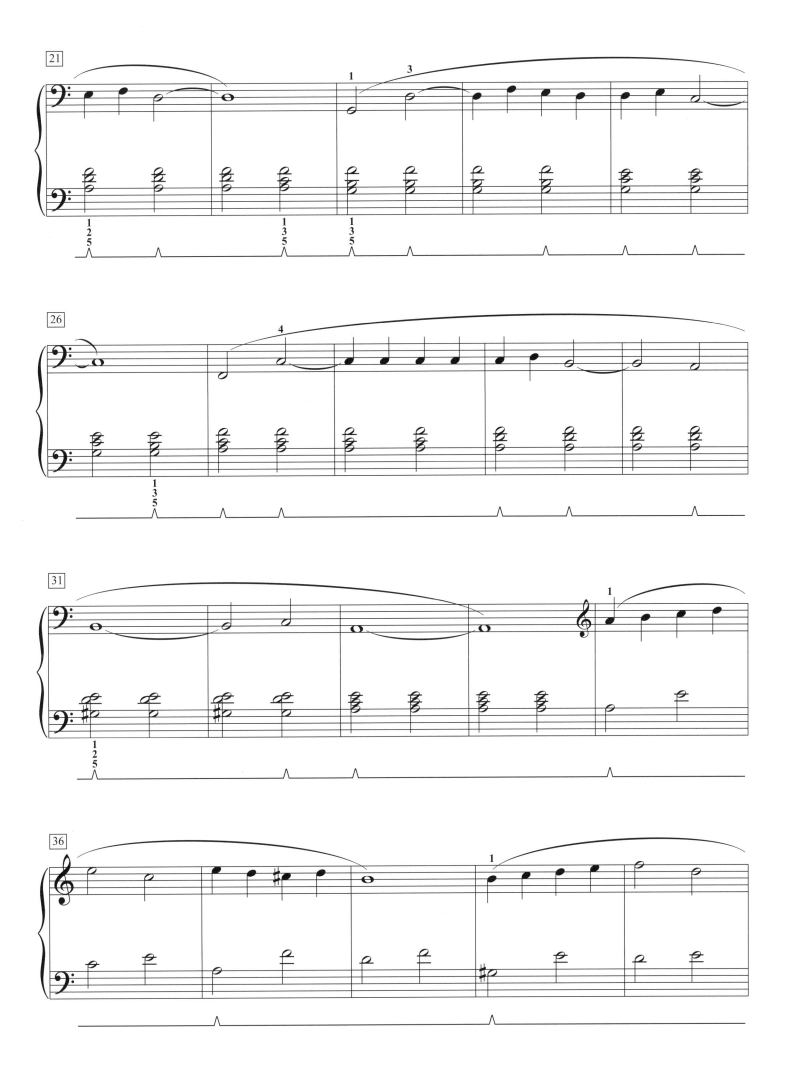

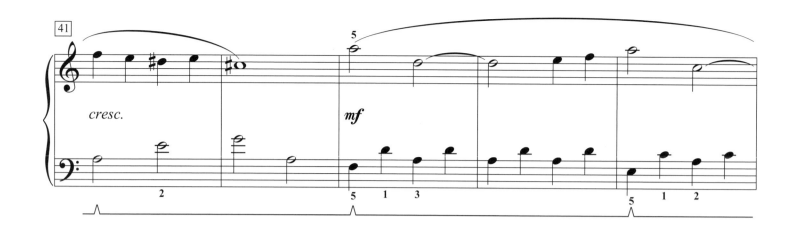

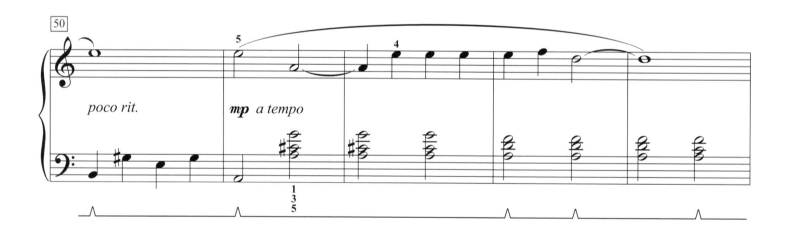

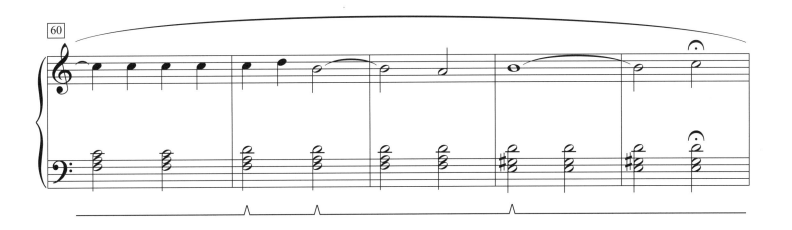

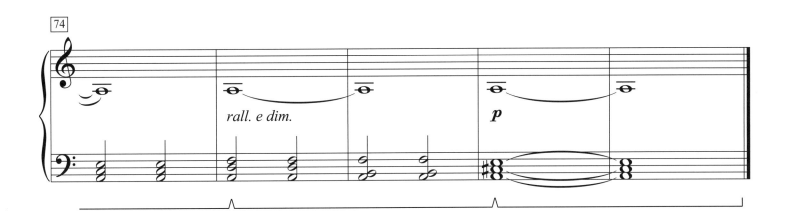

EARLY INTERMEDIATE

Nocturne

Mona Rejino

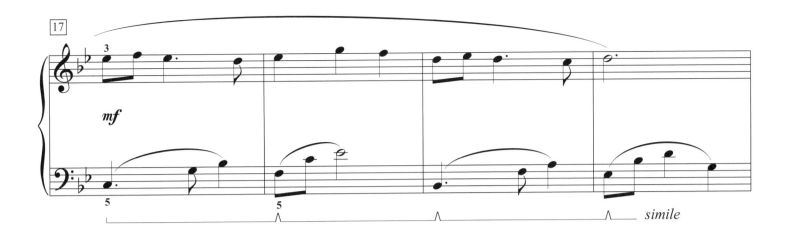

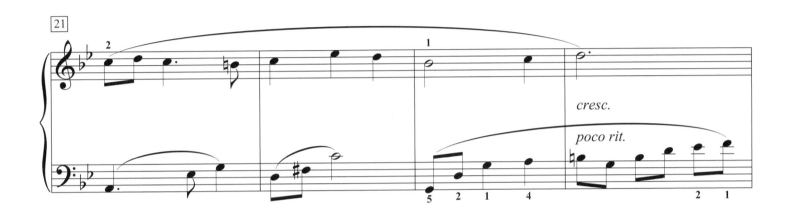

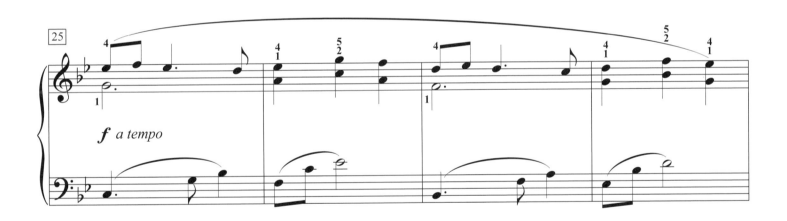

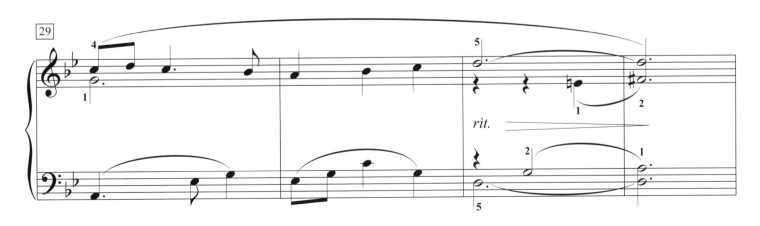

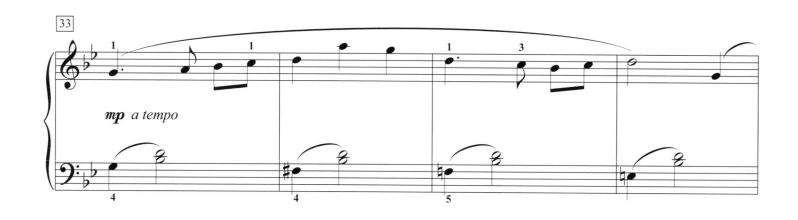

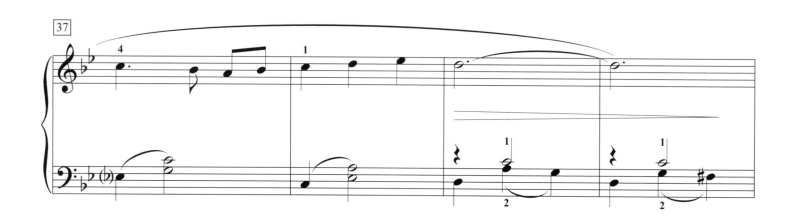

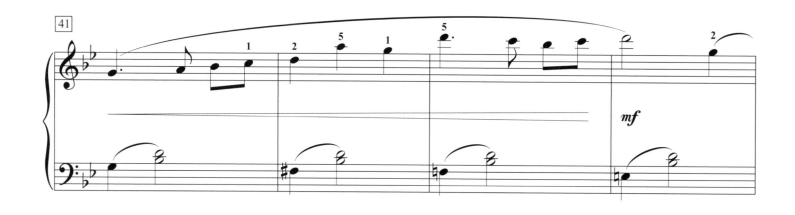

Tarantella

By Jennifer Linn

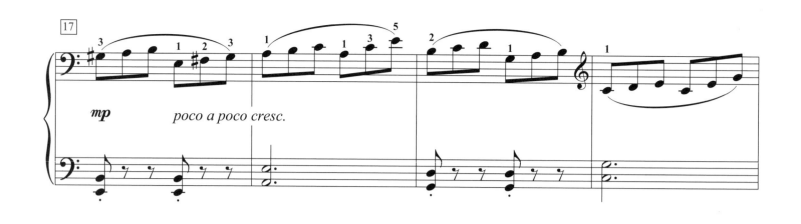

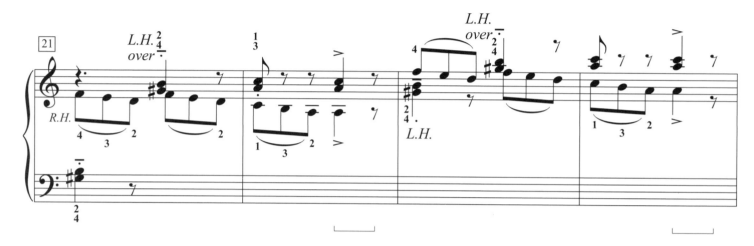

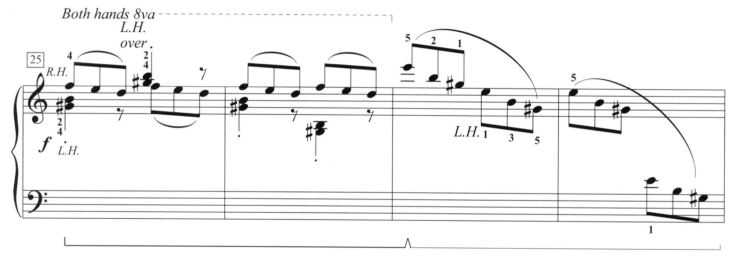

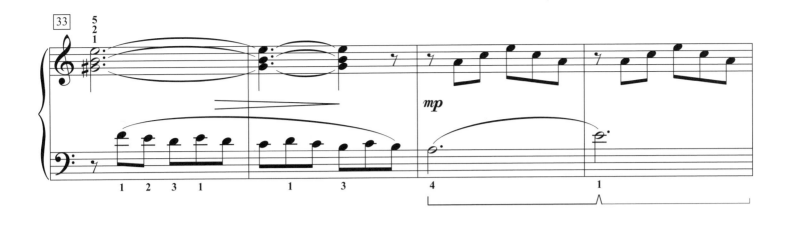

Petite Classique

By Phillip Keveren

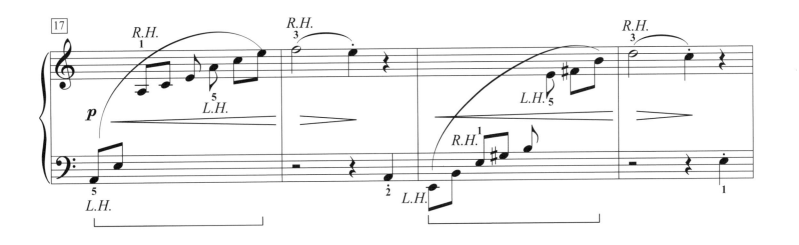

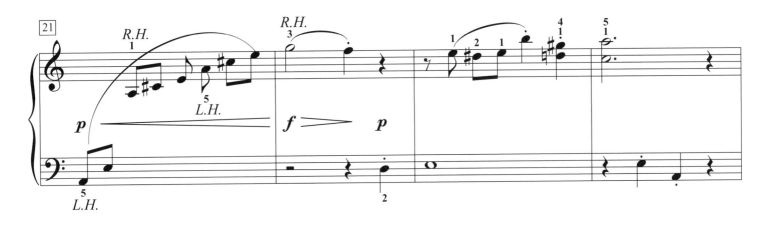

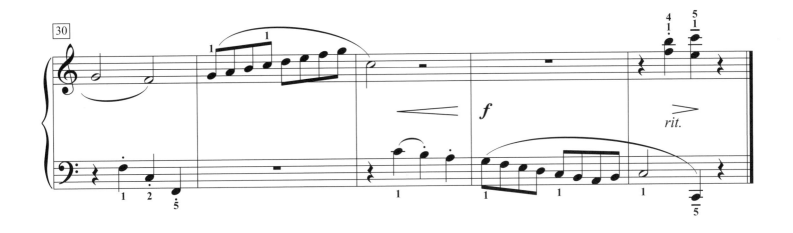

INTERMEDIATE

Dedicated to Lucy Laurain

Canon Fantasy

A Fantasy on Pachelbel's Canon in D

By Lee Galloway

Für Elise

By Ludwig van Beethoven
(1770–1827)
Arranged by Jennifer Linn

Jesu, Joy of Man's Desiring

from CANTATA NO. 147

Johann Sebastian Bach
(1685–1750)
Arranged by Fred Kern

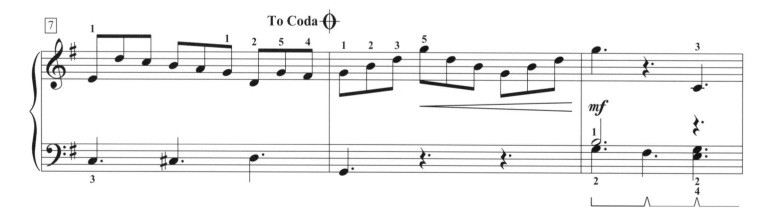

Nocturne Mystique

Jennifer Linn

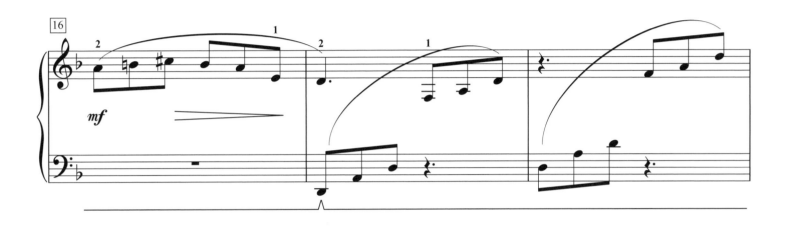

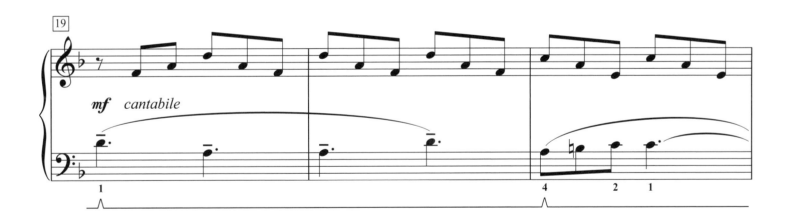

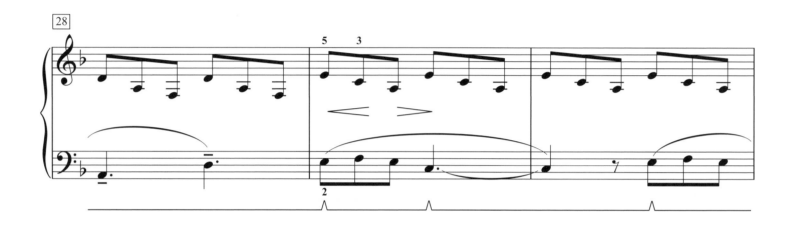

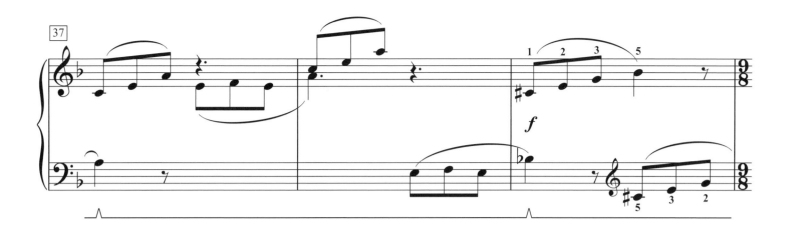

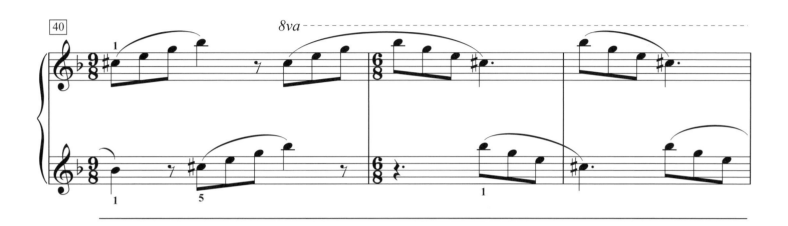

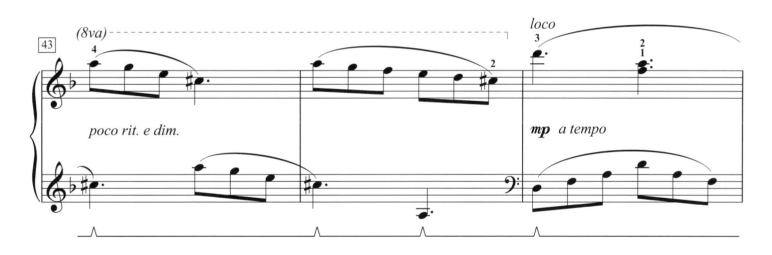

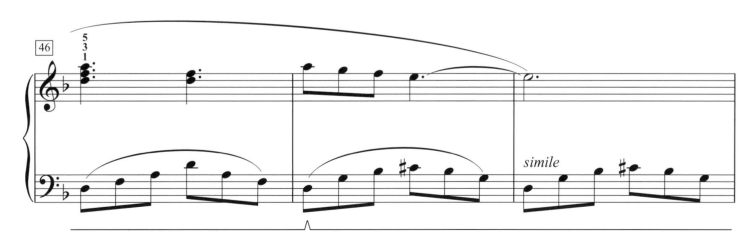

Sonatina Bravo

I

By Carol Klose

Allegro, in "2" (♩ = 88-96)

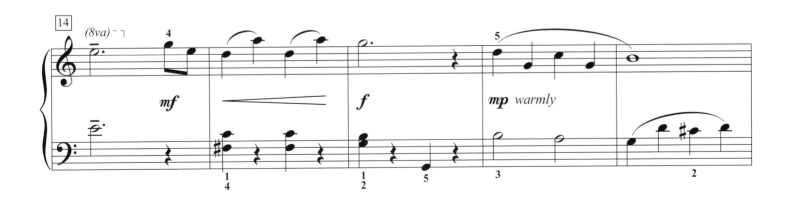

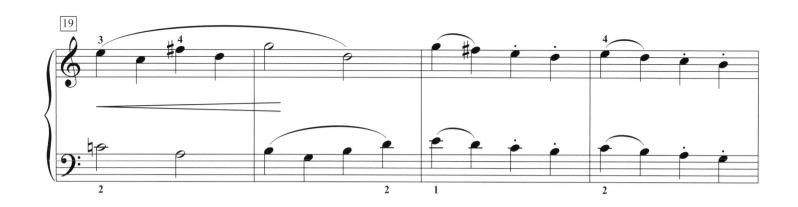

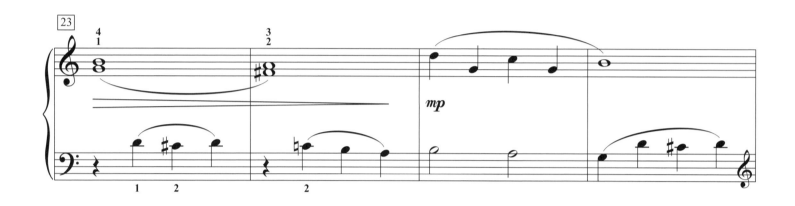

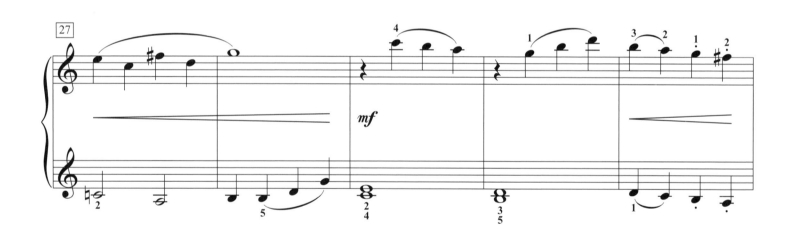

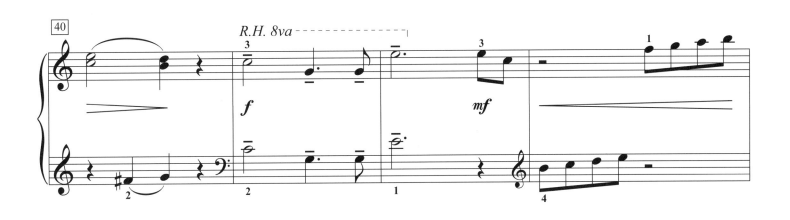

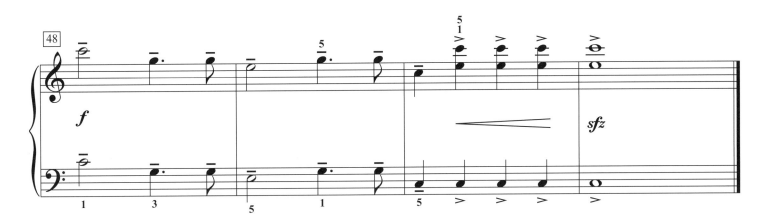

II

Andante cantabile (♩ = 120)

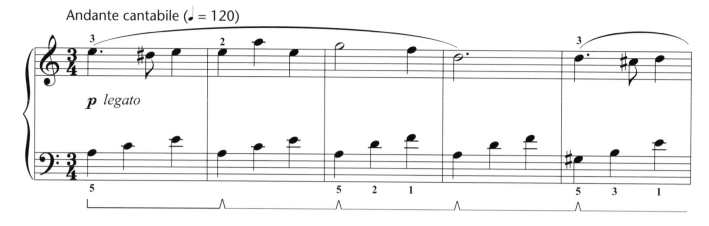

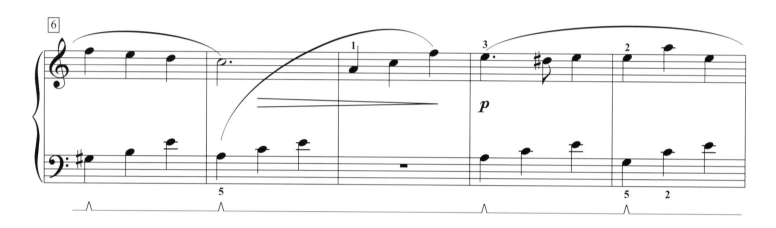

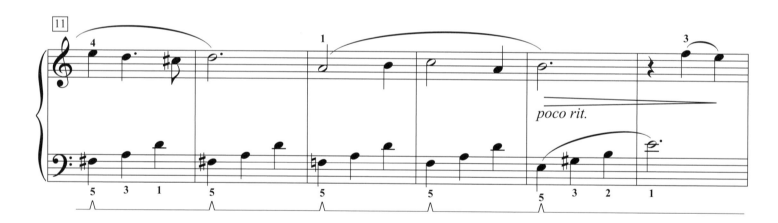

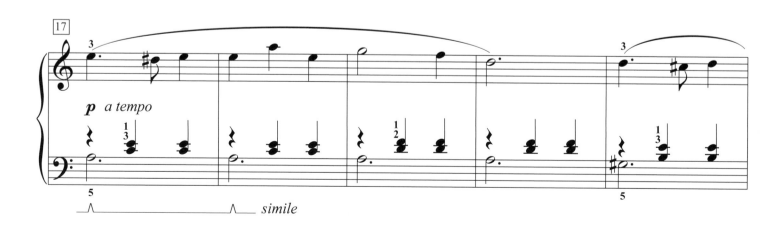

44

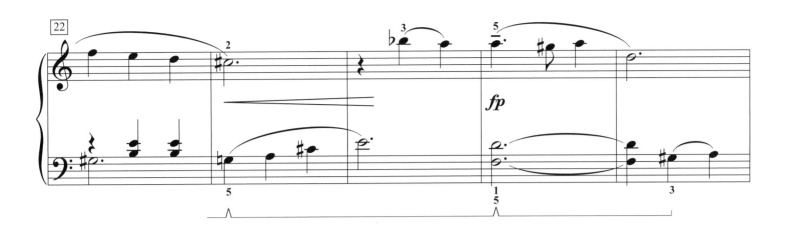

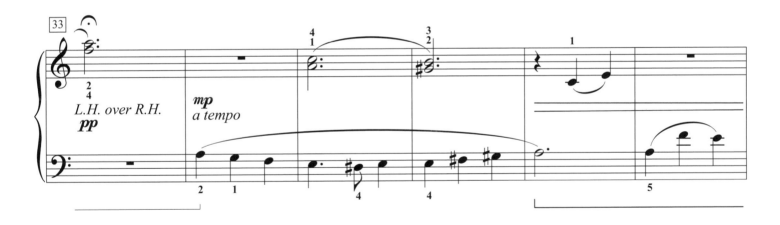

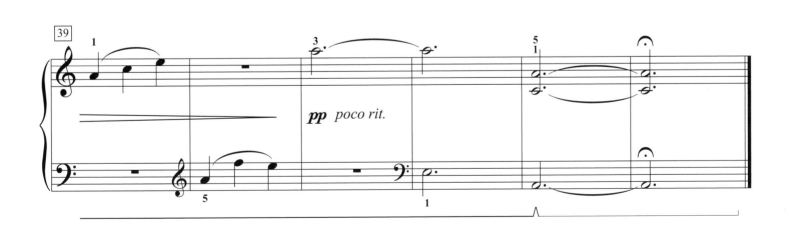

III

Scherzando vivace (♩ = 104-112)

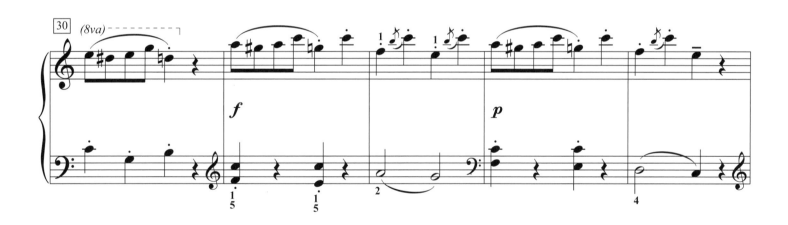

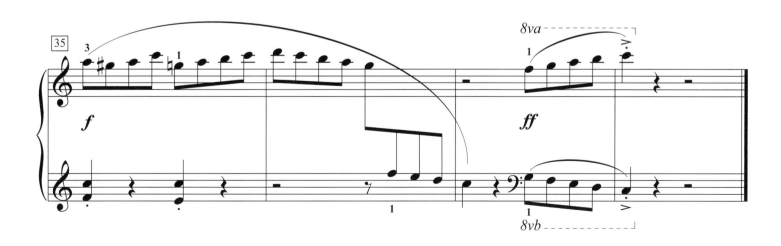

JOURNEY THROUGH THE
CLASSICS

COMPILED AND EDITED BY JENNIFER LINN

Journey Through the Classics is a four-volume piano repertoire series designed to lead students seamlessly from the easiest classics to the intermediate masterworks. The graded pieces are presented in a progressive order and feature a variety of classical favorites essential to any piano student's educational foundation. The authentic repertoire is ideal for auditions and recitals and each book includes a handy reference chart with the key, composer, stylistic period, and challenge elements listed for each piece. Quality and value make this series a perfect classical companion for any method.

BOOK 1 ELEMENTARY
00296870 Book Only...........................$6.99
00142808 Book/Online Audio........$8.99

BOOK 2 LATE ELEMENTARY
00296871 Book Only...........................$6.99
00142809 Book/Online Audio........$8.99

BOOK 3 EARLY INTERMEDIATE
00296872 Book Only...........................$6.99
00142810 Book/Online Audio........$8.99

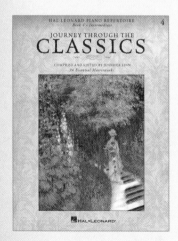

BOOK 4 INTERMEDIATE
00296873 Book Only...........................$7.99
00142811 Book/Online Audio........$9.99

**JOURNEY THROUGH
THE CLASSICS COMPLETE**
(all 4 levels included in one book)
00110217 Book Only.......................$17.99
00123124 Book/Online Audio.....$24.99

HAL•LEONARD®

www.halleonard.com

Prices, contents, and availability subject
to change without notice.